TABLE OF CONTENTS

For My mother,

You embedded the word of God in me since I was a child, and I pray, through this poetry book the Lord's word will be spread around the globe. I love you mommy!

Your *Gia B.*

My Child

My child will never see a cup to my mouth,
Unless it's juice or water, you see how I grew up.
You had to beg and barter, your dreams
Given to you in pennies, nickels, and dimes.
Yet your clothes matching with everything that rhymes...

My child will never see Mommy and Daddy fuss
Or fight; if we're gonna do this, we're gonna do it right.
My child, one whole, not pieces or parts, perfection
Is the goal. My child will know what it means to be loved
Beyond measure, husband and wife together!

My child will never worry about a touch between the legs,
Nah, not those thoughts in my babies' heads!
My child will never see what failure reaches to be,
They will see the highest level of me. Not some crazy running wild,
But a testimony with a smile—that will be my child...

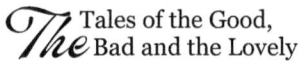
I Love You More

I love you more than words could say,
I love you more than yesterday,
More than the lilies singing in the trees...
Like that fresh Stocklin breeze,
I love you more than a caged bird singing its song.

I love you when it's right and even when you're wrong,
I love you when your smile is enough to shine through the moon,
Or when your soft cinnamon skin aligns to gleam every tune!
I love you more than the curly hairs on your head,

More than the fresh smell of banana bread,
And even more than the words that spread.
I've said I love you more each and every day,
And though times begin to grit and grim,
Just know I will always love you in and out of time.

Brown Girl

Oh, Brown girl, how much is owed to thee,
No matter how you try, they won't let you be,
Lifting the life in your skin, oh, how much you fight again!
With thick hair and shiny skin, it's the blood I feel
Within, my hair too big, my curls too tight, but too bad
Of what you feel 'cause I'm feelin' alright!

Crown high and mighty just as before.
Too bad all it does to you is bore, but for me, I like my crown
And all the secrets it holds, how it bounces when it's brushed!
And curls in its folds...

My skin may be brown, but it's soft like cinnamon,
And sweet like honey, not a product or to be bought
With money. This is genes and not the ones you buy at the store,
This is cinnamon sugar and a lot more... Oh, Brown girl, she's
second to none, look at her crown that shapes her as one.

Who Am I

The marvel, the muse, the thing,
Am I a bird with a broken wing or am I that thing,
That very ring waiting in someone's ear to change
Their tomorrow...

Am I an image of self-pity that's gone too far
Or am I a voice just waiting to scream my song,
For I am stuck in a vortex of time, I cannot escape,
Is it real or is it fake... I whisper to myself in the dead of night,
With no one around the room, quiet and sound, and that is where
I find my ground!

But for a minute I see all that I am to be,
For I am grateful, tall, dark, and strong,
And in that nothing is wrong. Who am I, I ask,
And other answers I sometimes may seek,
But I am exactly who I am meant to be, and that is me,
As loud and as poised as I'd like to be, with no penalty it's me.

Symphony

Still, quiet, no longer bound,
It's normally loud and busy, but right now you can hear.
Every sound, every laugh, every cry. No longer do I just say goodbye,
But hello to a better tomorrow, to a smile I've grown to know so well,
To a secret quiet place I know I can dwell.

For once in a blue moon, I can finally sing to a new tune,
Not a song of sorrow or a song of pain, but a song of cheers, and a smirk not in vain.
Feeling loud and brave, letting life time me with every wave!

For I am a daughter phenomenally,
A phenomenal daughter that is finally free,
Not having to worry or flee, for I found the key.
It is in thee, the one I worship and call Abba Father.
In you, I am safe and not bothered by the evil one,
Who tells me I'm all alone. In you, I know I have a firm foundation,
And a home!

Time

You can often feel late to the destination,
But I wonder how it's your own reservation,
A divine appointment by God set for you
That neither devil nor man can undo.
You may get weary and begin to cry,
But then stop to wonder why.

I have a gift that's like no other, not like my sister
Nor my brother. My gift has been anointed just for my hand;
I cannot be weak but stand! Sometimes it doesn't take
A lot of words or a complex phrase, but a word from God to set
The world ablaze...

You see, my friend, you are never late for your own
Destiny, so when you arrive it shall be pure ecstasy.
At that exact moment God said, "Here next to me,"
To dwell beside Him in perfect harmony,
Putting on the full cover of God's armory.
You see, time waits for no man, but it has no choice
When it comes to Jireh's plan.

I Am Not

First off, I would like to introduce myself as what and who I am.
Hello, I am your future president, senator, or even lawyer.
You may also call me your future professor and billionaire.
And oh, how some may grimace and stare...
But how quickly they forget God brought me there.
And even though it's hard, that in itself is enough.

You will provide me with respect and treat me as such,
And for that, I thank you very much. However,
You mustn't mistake me for things I am not.
I am not for sale, nor will I be bought.

I am not your maid, shoeshiner, or cook,
For I can speak, write, and read a book.
I am not your mammy or your wet nurse,
Your baker, or even your shoemaker.
I don't belong to massa or live in a shack.
I am intelligent, strong, and proud to be Black.
In moments, I may be timid, and sometimes a foe.
But most of all, I am NOT YOUR NEGRO.

Melanin

I am a woman made of melanin, hear my roar,
Watch me fly and see me soar.
Black is charm, Black is pain,
Black is the blood that runs through my veins.

Black is screaming to have a voice,
And working without a choice!
Black is the color of my hair,
And the labor my ancestors wear.
Black is beauty, Black is queen,

We all say this but what do we mean?
Black is being unapologetic without care,
So be proud of who you are, you beautiful,
Black heir.

Face

Beautiful brows that furrow on the side
Matching my deep coffee eyes, bright and wide
Down to my nose, large and strong, stemming from my ancestors
Who in them knew no wrong,

To my lips that have yet to be kissed by the depths of this life
To my temples, filled with pain and strife, each line telling a story of
Its own, secrets of the slaves finally gone home

To my wide ears that hear everything from here to the Mississippi
For I'm all good if it's all with me, my eyes, my nose, my forehead, I
Love it all, given by the ancestors making them feel tall
After the beating and blackening had ceased, one thing would
always be released

A praise to their God for making them exactly how He wanted them
to be, with hair like wool and lips on full, a big nose and ears to
match
For that is the one thing that they would not snatch, who they were
Was forever ingrained in their souls, smudging in the gap and filling
the holes

Here

So, um, here it goes,
I just have some feelings, some fears, some woes.
My worries lie not in what happens in a school day
But in my dreams, at night... when it's all tucked away.

A thousand screams of a lost daughter searching for her mother,
Being Black and feeling small is like no other,
For I carry the weight of my ancestors on my shoulders,
Splitting and tearing my skin like boulders.
The words the "man" has said to me,
Oh! How I just long to be free.

Giavonna puts on a brave face,
Trying her best to slide past this white human race.
But look! It's right here, the crack from the mask behind her left ear...
It starts small and runs deep, like the dried tears of a slave child
Screaming in his sleep...

But wait, she seems to be alright,
But what you don't see is that her grin is her fight.
For if her mouth closed and her smile faded,
She would be created, the marvel, the muse, the thing.
Her soul would glisten, and her spirit take wing.

However, all that blackness aside,
The scared little girl is still inside,
Afraid to come out and face the dawn,
Dreading all her security and sanity is gone.
Oh, how she yearns to cut the hurt and bleed her truths...
To stop time and relive her joyful young youths.

When life was simple and this dimension was clear,
Where she had no worry, no fear, she never cried
No tears, when playing was pleasant, and thoughts were clear,
But somehow she ended up here.

People

A continuation of the one before,
Except this time it will dig a little more.
A man seeps from a broken home, feeling alone—
"A real man doesn't cry," yells a man from the street.

Yet years later, it's his wife he begins to beat.
Pent-up feelings aren't good for the soul.
Not just the heart, but on the mind, they take a toll.

Or a woman, begging for help, off drugs,
Being told it's her fault, yet they were made to keep her in the vault,
Locked in a cave trying to escape,
Leaning in to cope in all the wrong ways.
So people, what do you have to say?

As you stand on trial, People v. Insanity
Has been the case all the while,
Yet we sit here and pretend nothing is wrong,
And yet the "American Dream" was unraveling all along.

Sanctuary

Oh, in you my heart I bury, is it true?
Are you my sanctuary, to have and to hold,
Whether it's meek or it's bold, it's my place to unfold.

We bow our heads and say Amen,
For no one we mean to offend.
Oftentimes we sit and tarry,
But isn't that the purpose of the sanctuary?

To sit, to ponder, to have random thoughts,
And to wonder, thinking about the unknown
And what is prone to happen in due time.
But not to worry, my child, it is all in line.

The prayers have many utterances,
And the languages may vary.
But isn't that the very purpose of the sanctuary?

I Am Woman

I am woman, I am the endangered species,
Yet I am not the victim, this is my story and I tell it well.
The oil is my life and I am the well,
I dance and sing all day long,
I am the bird, and my struggle is my song.

I am life and all that it holds,
Strife is the start, yet peace is the goal.
I am woman, I am the endangered species,
Here to claim back my throne. My skin is the mood,
And my words set the tone

For how my life will go and all the wonders that follow.
Yes, I may be endangered,
But that doesn't mean I have not savored
All the sorrowful goodbyes,
But it is time for me to forgive and get ready to fly.

Afraid

The Negro spirituals that brew inside,
The proud and praise of what's left behind.
In solitude, quiet—a place where I dwell,
And, in that, all is well.

The presence of prayer in a thousand different tongues!
The cry of the elders and the grief of the young.
Eyes closed, head bowed, posture upright and true—
In that stance, I give you all praise that is due.

The quiver of my lip, as exaltation,
And my tears as a representation.
A sealing to my amen, oh how I do that, again, again, and again—
The pulling of a person unknown.

For I am proud of how I've grown.
In pieces and spots of hole,
In the world I am broken, but in you I am whole!
For my debts can never be repaid, and in that, I am never afraid.

The planting of my feet and the sharpness of my shoulder,
For in You I can move mountains, rocks, and boulders.
Oh! How my spirit prays and calls out to Thee, for in You I am
free,
Darkness no longer shadowing, but light ahead,
For in You I am alive, no longer dead.

The crook of my bones screams a song like no other,
You, my friend who sits closer than a brother!
For this gift of the pen is none of my own,
It is You I give praise in every zone!

For every smile, word, and tone,
In You, the Creator of all...
You stand me upright, even when I fall.
I am not afraid of the valley, for that is where You called me,
Where anointing flows, and blind eyes see.
You will always be my Him in my every song,
For I am sometimes right, but You are never wrong...

All My Life

Since the beginning of my existence,
I have been the very bone of everyone's pain!
Yet my soul has always pulled for greater,
It was always now and never later.

Calm down, it don't take all that—
Yup, that's what was said!
But man, forget that, I need this bread.
And no, not the cheddar, the cheese, or the sauce,
'Cause no matter how much, you're never really a boss.
Wisdom is the end, and that you can't pretend.

Anybody can rent a car, but there's knowledge in the scar!
You know, the one you gave yourself when no one was looking.
You thought it was good, but it's actually hooking
Your soul on a pedestal; you cannot pay. "Go far and prosper"
Is all you can say, and yes, there is some gain and strife,
But it is still all my life.

The Beauty Of The Hood

Now we all know that one part of town where stuff just isn't good
It's formally known as the ghetto, but we call it the hood,
Where men are gunned down and taken from this life,
Where many families suffer from hunger, pain, and strife,
But what they don't say is it's all the good,

From loud church organ on Sunday mornin',
To the touch of sizzlin' hot comb without a warnin'!
To a mother that feels so warm, to the stopping of a bus
Or a cry of a newborn. The sound of a gun in the dead of night,
To a mother telling her children everythang is gonna be alright.

To the collard greens Big Momma makes so well
To the fruit market on the corner where apples and oranges is all they
sell,
To the music singing from street to street,
To the growing culture and the food to eat.
Man, there is nothing like the hood, some things may be wrong but it's
still all good,

My hood, the place that I call home where my spirit is me and my love
does roam.
It's all good, my hood, much is ode to thee
For in you we can be one as well as be free.
It's all good, my hood, if only they knew the joy you bring,
Where our freedom can fly and a caged bird can sing.

Used By You

So many in culture may fail, fall, and falter,
But you, Abba, made me to build an altar
For your glory and honor alone, not to post or "tag" on a phone.
I was created to be the head, a holy nation, and a peculiar
people,
Not a curb, but a steeple. Oh, how society still makes it seem my
fault when YOU created me to be salt.

Yet people still desire for glam and fortune,
But demons tremble at the very mention of your name.
Though you never have a big social page or a blue check by your
name,
Your following changed the game, for generations still
implement your practices, and to me that's more valuable than
influencers and actresses.

For you, Father, knew me before I was formed and fashioned in
my mother's womb. In that, you knew my gift and made room,
setting me apart from the others and clothing me in the
uniqueness of true. For in my mind, your word is forever stuck
like glue. Oh, how I desire to be used by you.

It's Ok

As a Christian, I am often looked at as
A hypocrite, and even crazy.
Not because of my own doing or being lazy,
But from the impression of my "religion."
For in culture, it's left a deep incision
That punctured deep in the heart of man,
Leaving him to make a "plan."

When that was never the case,
For it was God's job to save the human race.
But instead of running to Him, we ran from,
And right into the arms of the evil one.
Now to become a woman can be bought,
But that is not how I was taught.
And yet we were His promise as pride. I mean, come on,
Do we truly have to hide?

According to my Father, the answer's no,
We don't have to hide from our wounds, for He's close
To the brokenhearted, and even those we seem departed.
In all our shame and guilt, it is still our lives He built.
For in His own supernatural way,
With arms wide, He'll still say it's okay.

Moved By You

Oh, the secrets your voice releases,
Filling in the lines and gapping the creases.
Your words touch my soul in a way's control—
How comforting are your words, my love,
Seeping deep in my spirit, leading me to yearn
So all can hear it.

Your lines tracing my being like no hands touched before,
Your tone and pitch, leading me to want more.
Your style and your groove, I'll always be in tune with,
For you are a living verse, a phrase, and never a myth.

For your warmth shall never leave, and your tenderness never fade,
For you grow like wine, just better with age.
How careful you are with my heart, for you and I shall never part,
An ode to poetry who is forever true, oh,
How I am moved by you.

My Name Ain't

My breasts aren't for your pleasure or perverted gaze.
They were given to my ancestors to make it through this maze,
To nurse my children and birth the next generation—
Not to grope or squeeze for your infatuation!

I refuse to be distorted or contorted in devious sexual ways,
Especially not for a man's raging sexual blaze.
I shall not become embedded in the dresser as did the female
slave,
Her skin aching, and screech ready to pop as she begs and begs
Massa to stop.

That is why I've come to speak for the little slave girl who never
had a voice,
To finally give her what she never had—a choice
In how she speaks, and even her flame,
For that was always kept in a milky frame.

Yet the secret is I am the slave, to what this society thinks of me,
Instead of embracing all that I was meant to be.
And if you ask me my name, I may hesitate in just a thought,
But will be quick to tell you what it is not.

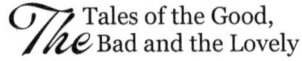
My name ain't, "Aye ma with the big booty,"
"Hey Queen," "Hi love," or "Sup lil cutie."
My name ain't *puts phone in hand*
And especially not *grabs me with a weighted demand.*

For I am a daughter of the Most High
And in that, there is no question of why.
I exude virtue, and you will treat me with such,
And for that, I thank you oh so much.
For I serve a God who heals and closes sores,
So I've come to tell you my name ain't yours.

Somebody

Ever since I was a little girl, I thought it came from above
That simple phrase, the four-letter word, and some call it love
The patient thing, the one that is forever kind
But somehow, I'm always left behind

Now don't get me wrong, I have every reason to
But sometimes I just don't know what to do
For a word so short, it takes the longest to say
Whether I've known you for a lifetime or just yesterday

You know, that love jones
With little secrets and quiet moans
And no, not sexual, but purely intellectual
Oh, how the stimulation of the mind is like no other
Especially in the warm embrace of each smother

A deep stroke to the cerebellum,
So, keep quiet; we don't have to tell 'em
For how we wonder is private to us
Therefore, no one can make a fuss
For I don't want anything dirty or naughty
But to listen and learn from somebody

Misunderstood

You know your intelligence, yet ignorance is quite infuriating.
I used to feel sorry for you, but now I'm debating:
Is it the real you, or is this all just an act?
'Cause you know I've always wondered, as a matter of fact.

The tides and waves of what make you who you are—
Were you born this way, or has life dimmed your star?
Have the seams of life left you this jaded,
Or is it all your life to be free you just waited?

To tell your story and bleed your truths,
To smile, laugh, and relive your youths—
And not the ones that snatched the little girl all too soon,
But the ones that watered her and awaited her to bloom.

For I know now why you operate the way you do,
Yet it is no fault to blame you.
You are only remaining to what is true,
And although you grin and say, "It's all good,"
At the end of the day, you're simply misunderstood.

You Can Make It

The groove and hustle sours over time
Grit, the move, and always on that grind
The dirt under your nails, the testament of how far you've come,
for you know with the Lord the fixed fight is already won

The growl in your belly deepens with every groan for that hunger
in your soul calling to go home, the land that flows with milk and
honey, and although you had no money
You always had the one true God
Even when things were shaky and odd

You could always count on Jehovah to give more, to lift your
wings, pour in courage, and allow you to soar, even when hands
were bloody and minds tainted, the weak never got weary, and the
good never fainted

For it's been anchored in our minds: with God, all things are
possible, which is true, but you have to jump that obstacle, not
people's opinions and what society says
But focusing on the Father instead

For the pain of the journey may linger,
Just know God knows you to the point of your very finger.
He created you in all your complexities,
So trust He will give you all the necessities,
To get to the very top where He wants you to be,
Serving Him, and finally free.

So take the journey, enjoy the twists and turns of every road,
Knuckle down, suck it up, and get in that mode,
For with the Lord there is no need to fake it
And always know you can make it.

Firm Foundation

The one who never wavers, fails, or crumbles
Even when I may trip, fall, and stumble
You forever remain solid, steadfast, and immovable,
For in you all sins and blemishes are removable

All because you sacrificed that precious blood we have been
singing about for centuries, for it matters not the wage or density,
because in you we are created a creature, a new creation, and that
I shall scream aloud to every nation

For I am not ashamed of the Gospel of Jesus Christ,
No matter the pain, misery, or strife
In you I have all freedom and life
Even in my darkest moments you knew me and cared,
Even if a tear is all that I shared

For you, Father, know me like no other,
You are the friend that sits closer than a brother
For without you there can be extreme hesitation,
But never when I stand on the firm foundation

Teach Me

Lord, I must admit, I need guidance with this part,
For it's not a simple issue, but matters of the heart.
I've rarely seen it done in the right way,
Except, of course, when You gave Your life away.
You did and rose for the world to be,
To live, to flourish, and to be free.

So, I guess I seek a more humanly view,
Like how You love a brother, a father, or even a mother too,
Not just when all is well, but when smiles are rare,
And emotions are tangled, with burdens to bear.

Show me how to wield the fruits of the Spirit,
Infused with Your profound love,
For living that way is a gift from above.
Lord, guide me to love even when they frustrate me endlessly,
When they keep nagging or won't let me be.

And one more thing, if You would,
Teach me to trust and perceive as I should,
Not just the butterflies and the sweet,
But the vinegar in one's soul,
So I stay whole,
And not broken by folly that wasn't me.
Oh God, please guide me.

Me & U

The Tales of the Good, the Bad, and the Lovely

Oh, how our connection is like no other,
Yet it is not a choke or a smother.
For you sit high and look low,
But never appear as an enemy or foe.

You sharpen my mind for the battles ahead,
To conquer, crush, and instill dread,
Against the true adversary I face,
Cutting through deceit with grace.
Though his lies are not from you, they can't prevail,
For only your truth can truly impale the heart.
Though the enemy's seeds may seem to start,
It's only as much as you allow,
And that I'll always avow.

For you, oh God, grant me reason and rhyme,
You, Holy One, who holds and shapes time.
Yet you move within and beyond its space,
And for that reason, I shall never lose pace.
The time He created, He doesn't even live within,
Driving me to awaken, to rise, and begin.

Jireh, I celebrate who you are and all you achieve,
Constantly guiding me out and helping me believe.
For I possess strength, despite what I pursue,
I'd lose my mind if not for you.
Particularly, if you weren't keeping me whole like glue,
So, here's to an everlasting bond—me and you.

I Won't Complain

Lord, You know what's best for me
Even when my earthly eyes can't see
Even when I don't comprehend
I trust You'll never let go of my hand
And so, I thank You, Lord,
For I can't afford to follow my own accord

So, I will praise Your name amid my trials
For I know my own efforts are futile
When everything falls apart and I'm lost
You're there, even when life seems unjust
When friends and people stray away
I know in You, I'll always find my way

You wipe my tears and calm my fears
You pray when all I can do is groan
In You, I dwell; my heart is Your home
So even in the depths of pain
Lord, I promise I won't complain

Your Temple

Oh, what an honor it is to be
A place where You dwell, and my soul is free.
No longer bound by the chains holding me,
For You, Father, abide in me and I in You.
So I shall never worry about what to do,
I know in my spirit I can always turn to Thee,
For when I call on You, demons flee.

Even in my time of despair,
I know You will always be there.
Day by day I strive to produce fruit,
To be pleasing unto You, not to be cute.
For I find peace in Your presence alone,
In You I have a friend, Father, and home.
Thank You for not counting me out when I didn't feel
like enough,
For You knew I was still composed of the right stuff.

Yet it was none of me, so don't assume
It was He who knew me before my mother's womb
And even with all my crooks and flaws
You still gave me a because
Because You lived, I shall not die
Because You heal, I have reason why
That's the reason it is a privilege and honor
To forever be a temple of the Father

Still

It is a common misconception you can't always hear God,
So, let's think, is this true or is it really a façade?
For the Father is always speaking, but are we listening is the question.
Are we using all the tools and guides in our possession,
Or are we too focused on how to make it to the next blessing?

Not realizing the true lesson is the pasture,
And if we focused on that, the "next" would come "faster."
Not our definition of the word of force,
But God's, for He is the author of every course.
He is also the great finisher, through and through,
So, stop trying to "fix it" with white-out or glue.

For in our eyes the story is messy and distorted,
But to God, it's perfect, so chill—He'll restore it.
Yet only the parts that need it, of course,
Because some things we must learn, not force.
So in all your ways acknowledge Him, seeking His will.
Dive into the Word, get quiet, and be still.

God Made

Let's talk about a topic that always seems to vex:
Not gossip or envy—yup, you guessed it—sex.
I know, I know, the topic seems so taboo,
Yet what if it's not? But really, it's me and you...
Making a God-given act seem so perverted,
Something so precious, be nasty, and misworded.

For that's what happens when the world injects it into a
child's mind,
Now, the innocence and purity apparently left behind.
All from an image seen by a child of six,
Now it is her mind and body she is left to "fix."
Yet little does she know it didn't even start with her,
It started with generations before causing this blur.

The devil just so happened to catch her young,
Trying to ensure that then the damage was done.
Distorting her view of sex and temple forever,
But little does he know she pursues God in every
endeavor.
So, the image of sex was never ruined, just distorted,
But it's okay, for God is teaching her how to restore it,
Showing her it is only to be done under the covenant of
marriage.

That was she ain't 18, unmarried with a baby carriage
So please listen, hear God's warning, and take heed
Stay persistent on the path of virtue so the devil can't
mislead
For our bodies are not our own, so not with just anyone can
they be laid
So, sex is a pure activity that should only be done in the way
God made

The 'Safe' Sin

The next topic of today shall be the safe sin
Although it may not always come from within
Stemming from generations before and now a part of your story
But it's okay, we will learn, correct, and give God all the glory
So bear with me in these next moments, for they may bring hesitation
As we discuss the unfortunate topic of masturbation

A subject that the Church has neglected for years
Leaving some of us broken, and most in tears
Not knowing how to pry off something that once brought comfort
While not truly knowing the consequences under the dirt
For the mental torment it brings is all too real
So truly in the end, it's not just orgasm you feel

But the shame and condemnation that come in like a flood
Yet do not worry, my child, it is covered by my blood
So, turn and repent, thus says the Lord
Flee from the enemy and use your sword!
For there is no condemnation for those in Christ Jesus
So no matter how you feel, God never leaves us
That's why we must go to His word whenever we face temptation
Be wise with who we call friends, and allow for ventilation
Please, boys and girls, we must allow God to heal us from within
So, put the phone down, turn Jesus up, and RUN from the "safe" sin

He's Able

A statement often used in Black church
Posted on social media and put even on merch
However, it doesn't mean God will just do it
But He'll feel every emotion and help you through it
The good, the bad, and everything in between
So don't ever feel ignored, because you are seen!

For the God above, He is able to feel it all
Whether it is small, wide, big, or tall
He doesn't just deliver and ignore your pain
So no matter the trial, it is never in vain
God understands the heartache and suffering too
But always remember, it was even worse than you

Beaten and bruised just so we could attempt to get it right
So how dare you stand aside and not put up a fight!
Sitting here crying because they talked about you...
While Jesus got flogged so the future could be true
Now don't get me wrong, I'm not saying He doesn't care
Because that is not real, and He will always be there
He can relate like no one, so you never have to tell a fable
So, in that, know the Lord is always able!

Worth More Than Rubies

Babygirl, you don't have to display your breasts to feel loved,
For that feeling shall only come from God above.
You don't have to open your legs to feel happy and whole,
Because to be a woman of virtue should be the only goal.
So, there is no need to expose every section of skin,
For the Lord values not the outside, but what lies within.

Babygirl, you don't have to put on a full face to feel beautiful,
For in Christ, you were created fearfully and wonderful.
No need to be promiscuous to advance a male gaze,
You were created by the Highest to set the world ablaze!
So be the example for others, in how you talk and dress,
Becoming more of God, and little of the world, less and less.

And there is no shame in remaining pure,
Not just for marriage but only the Lord.
It's okay to say no, and reject what seems like gold,
Because that even runs in lies, and stories of old.
So, to my ladies, the ones that feel lacking in beauties,
Remember, you, a woman of virtue, is worth more than rubies!

Here Part 2

Oh, my God, You have done it again!
And how I praise You for being more than a friend.
Lord, for nobody but You can do like You do,
Again and again, You continue to pull me through!
In all that dirt, You saw a flower waiting to bloom,
And for that, I shall worship You until the tomb.

For, Lord, You are higher than any other,
And as always, You are a friend that sits closer than a brother.
Yet there are no words to describe how good You are;
Out of all the English language, You are oh so far...
Honestly, writing about You doesn't even equate to Your greatness.
Time and time again, You forever prove Your unwavering
faithfulness!

Because of that, there shall never be a need to fear,
For not only have You brought me from, but You've placed me here:
A sound place where You and the Father dwell,
And in that, all is well!

Yes, Jesus Loves Me

Oh, my God, You have done it again!
And how I praise You for being more than a friend.
Lord, for nobody but You can do like You do,
Again and again, You continue to pull me through!
In all that dirt, You saw a flower waiting to bloom,
And for that, I shall worship You until the tomb.

For Lord, You are higher than any other,
And as always, You are a friend that sits closer than a brother.
Yet there are no words to describe how good You are,
Out of all the English language, You are oh so far...
Honestly, writing about You doesn't even equate to Your
greatness.
Time and time again, You forever prove Your unwavering
faithfulness!

Because of that, there shall never be a need to fear,
For not only have You brought me from, but You've placed me
here,
A sound place where You and the Father dwell,
And in that, all is well!

"But each day the Lord pours his unfailing love upon me, and through each night I sing his songs, praying to God who gives me life."

Psalms 42:8 NLT

The Tales of the Good, Bad and the Lovely

ISBN 979-8-9916585-6-0

Published by ICXII Publishing
9570 Regency Square Blvd, Jacksonville, FL 32225 USA
Copyright © 2025 Giovanna Lee Suber. All Rights Reserved